WHY DO ANIMALS LiVE THERE?

Jonathan Rosen

Rourke
Educational Media

rourkeeducationalmedia.com

*Scan for Related Titles
and Teacher Resources*

Teaching Focus:
Using Expression- Have students read aloud to practice reading with expression and with appropriate pacing.

Before Reading:

Building Academic Vocabulary and Background Knowledge
Before reading a book, it is important to set the stage for your child or student by using pre-reading strategies. This will help them develop their vocabulary, increase their reading comprehension, and make connections across the curriculum.

1. Read the title and look at the cover. *Let's make predictions about what this book will be about.*
2. Take a picture walk by talking about the pictures/photographs in the book. Implant the vocabulary as you take the picture walk. Be sure to talk about the text features such as headings, Table of Contents, glossary, bolded words, captions, charts/diagrams, and Index.
3. Have students read the first page of text with you then have students read the remaining text.
4. Strategy Talk – use to assist students while reading.
   - Get your mouth ready
   - Look at the picture
   - Think…does it make sense
   - Think…does it look right
   - Think…does it sound right
   - Chunk it – by looking for a part you know
5. Read it again.
6. After reading the book complete the activities below.

Content Area Vocabulary
Use glossary words in a sentence.

amplified
burrow
colonies
immune
predators
venomous

After Reading:

Comprehension and Extension Activity
After reading the book, work on the following questions with your child or students in order to check their level of reading comprehension and content mastery.

1. *What are the advantages of animals that live or build their nests in trees?* (Summarize)
2. *How do Emperor penguins stay warm in the cold Antarctic climate?* (Asking questions)
3. *Why do some animals have relationships with other animals to help them survive?* (Text to self connection)
4. *Why are the senses of animals that live in caves amplified?* (Inferring)

Extension Activity
Animals live in different types of homes just like people! Pick out an animal you read about in the book and do some further research on their habitat, what they eat, if they are predator or prey, and what adaptations they use to hide or camouflage themselves. Record your findings in a notebook. Beside the animal facts, draw a picture of the animal. Observe other animals around your home and see if they have any similarities to the animals in the book.

Table of Contents

Home, Sweet Home

People live in homes for shelter and safety. Animals do too!

Alligators **burrow** under mud banks, up to 20 feet (6 meters) deep, using their snouts and tails.

Be careful where you dig, alligators don't like houseguests!

Rabbits burrow into the ground for shelter and protection against **predators.**

Burrowing owls don't like to do the hard work. They move into tunnels left by other animals.

Animals make their homes close to food sources. Groundhogs like to live near fence lines of vegetable crops. They also have many escape tunnels, in case one entrance is attacked.

Gophers live underground almost all of the time. They can dig tunnels up to 700 yards (640 meters) long. Thousands of gophers may live in one of these tunnels.

Tree Dwellers

Koalas dwell in trees. Their homes high up in the air protect them from predators on the ground.

Birds build nests in trees. This keeps their eggs safe from many animals that might eat them.

Raccoons like to live inside hollowed-out trees.

Raccoons are eating machines. They need fat reserves to give them energy and warmth through the winter months.

Many types of monkeys live in trees. They use vines or branches to swing from tree to tree.

Living in a Cave

Bat **colonies** sleep in caves during the day. They do their hunting at night. They choose cave homes near food and water sources.

Bats make high-pitched squeaking noises to help them find food. The sound bounces off nearby objects and tells the bat where things are located. This is called echolocation.

Some animals spend their entire lives inside caves. The olm is an amphibian, which eats, sleeps, and breeds in underwater caves.

Olms are blind because they live in total darkness. Their other senses, such as hearing and smell, are **amplified** to help them find food.

Portable Homes

Some animals like their homes so much, they take them everywhere they go. Hermit crabs live in shells. They move into bigger shells as they grow.

Turtles live in shells, too. Their shells grow with them as they get older.

Brrrr, It's Cold!

Some animals love the cold. Emperor penguins live in Antarctica, the coldest place on Earth. They have a warm layer of feathers. They also huddle together for warmth.

The male Emperor penguin sits on eggs for more than two months, in icy winds and storms, while the female goes off in search of food.

Polar bears split time between the water and the sea ice. They hunt from the sea ice. They also take naps on it!

Under the Sea

Lobsters live on the ocean floor, not far from the shoreline. They spend most of their lives hidden under rocks or burrowed in the sand and mud.

Some animals have relationships with other creatures to help them survive. Clownfish live in a **venomous** anemone.

Clownfish do a wiggling dance against the poisonous tentacles of the anemone. This helps them become **immune** to it. Underwater predators won't go after the clownfish because they are scared of the anemone.

Photo Glossary

amplified (AM-pluh-fyed): To make something louder or stronger.

burrow (BUR-oh): A tunnel or hole in the ground made or used as a home by an animal.

colonies (KAH-luh-nees): A large group of animals, of the same type, living closely together.

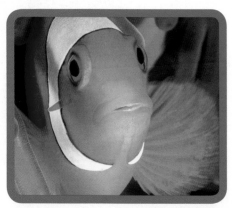
immune (IH-myoon): Protected from physical or emotional harm.

predators (PRED-uh-turz): Animals that live by hunting other animals for food.

venomous (VEN-uh-mus): Able to inflict a poisonous bite or sting.

Index

Meet The Author!
www.meetREMauthors.com

Websites to Visit

kids.nationalgeographic.com/animals

a-z-animals.com

www.nwf.org/Kids/Ranger-Rick/Animals.aspx

About the Author

Jonathan Rosen is a writer living in Coral Springs, Florida, with his family. He coaches his children in sports and helps them with their homework. Well, except for math, because that's really hard. He has lived all over the world and hopes to eventually find a place that will let him stay.

Library of Congress PCN Data

Why Do Animals Live There?/ Jonathan Rosen
ISBN 978-1-68191-722-1 (hard cover)
ISBN 978-1-68191-823-5 (soft cover)
ISBN 978-1-68191-917-1 (e-Book)
Library of Congress Control Number: 2016932646

Rourke Educational Media
Printed in the United States of America, North Mankato, Minnesota

Edited by: Keli Sipperley
Cover design, interior design and art direction:
Nicola Stratford   www.nicolastratford.com

PHOTO CREDITS: Cover © Chase Clausen; page 4 © Frank Fennema, Page 5 © Alligator© Eric Isselee, burrow © Holly Kuchera; Page 6 © Patryk Kosmider; page 7 © Mauricio S Ferreira; page 8 © LaurieSH; page 9 © Nuk2013; page 10 © Alvov; page 11 © Ondrej Prosicky; page 12 © Scenic Shutterbug; page 13 © nattanan726; page 14 © All-stock-photos; page 15 © Nacionalni park Una (Wikipedia); page 1 © davemhuntphotography; page 17 © Galina Savina; page 19 © Christopher Wood; page 20 © Ethan Daniels; page 21 © Suwat Sirivutcharungchit; page 23 bottom © Bill Kennedy. All photos from Shutterstock.com except page 15

Also Available as:

ROURKE'S
e-Books